PROMISE
OF
GOOD THINGS

The Apostolic Fathers

The Spirituality of the Fathers

3

PROMISE
OF
GOOD THINGS

The Apostolic Fathers

edited by
Oliver Davies

translated by
Alun Idris Jones and Oliver Davies

introduction by
Sheila Cassidy

New City Press
New Rochelle, New York

Published in the United States by New City Press
86 Mayflower Avenue, New Rochelle, New York 10801
©1993 New City, London, Great Britain

Translations by Alun Idris Jones and Oliver Davies

Library of Congress Cataloging-in-Publication Data:

Apostolic Fathers (Early Christian collection). English.
   Promise of good things : the Apostolic Fathers ; edited by
Oliver Davies ; translated by Alun Idris Jones and Oliver Davies ;
introduction by Sheila Cassidy.
                (The Spirituality of the Fathers ; 3)
   Includes bibliographical references.
   ISBN 1-56548-019-8 : $7.95
   1. Christian literature—Early–Greek authors. I. Davies,
Oliver. II. Jones, Alun Idris. III. Title. IV. Series.
BR60.A62   1993
270.1—dc20   92-42033

Printed in the United States of America

Contents

Introduction 7

A Note on the Apostolic Fathers 17

The Didache 21

The Two Ways — 23; The Way of Life/I — 25; The Way of Life/II — 26; The Eucharist: How to Give Thanks — 28; The Eucharist: Prayer of Thanksgiving — 29; The Eucharist: How to Approach It — 30

The Letter of Barnabas 31

Spiritual Counsel — 33; Spiritual Meditation — 35; The Temple of God — 36; The Way of Light — 38; Be Faithful — 41

The Shepherd 43

The Angel of Repentance — 45; First Commandment — 47; Second Commandment — 48; Fifth Commandment — 49; Tenth Commandment — 50; Twelfth Commandment — 51

Clement's First Letter to the Corinthians 53

The Glorious Rule of Tradition — 55; Humility of Spirit — 56; Hasten to God — 57; God's Promises — 60; How to Receive God's Gifts — 61; Christ, the Way — 62; The Army of God — 63; Serving the Common Good — 65; Opening the Heart's Eyes to God — 66; A Blessing — 67

Clement's Second Letter to the Corinthians . . 69

God's Mercy — 71; Detachment from the World — 72; Commitment — 73; The Virtue of Repentance — 74; God the Healer — 75; The Blasphemy We Provoke — 76; The True Church — 77; Encouraging One Another — 78; A Personal Prayer — 79; Complete Conversion — 80

The Letters of Ignatius 81

To the Magnesians: The Basic Choice in Life — 83; II/Living in Harmony with God — 84; III/Unity of the Body — 85; To the Romans:

Dying to the World — 86; II/Christian Strength — 87; III/God's Wheat — 88; IV/Dying and Living in Christ — 89; To the Philadelphians: Unity Protection from Evil — 90; II/Becoming Perfect for God — 91; III/The Discernment of the Spirit — 92; IV/Christ, Basis of Faith — 93; To the Smyrnaeans: The Mind of God — 94; To Polycarp: Cherish Unity — 95; Words to Polycarp's Community — 96

The Letter of Polycarp to the Philippians . . . 97

Suffering for Christ — 99; A Prayer — 100

The Letter to Diognetus 101

The Christian Life — 103; Christians are the Soul of the World — 105; The Coming of Christ — 106; The Mercy of God — 108; God's Imitators — 110; Love and Knowledge — 112

Short Bibliography 115

Introduction

I should never, ever, have said yes to Oliver Davies when he asked me to write an introduction to this book. I am not a theologian and I knew next to nothing about the Apostolic Fathers until a few weeks ago. So why on earth did I agree to do it, I ask myself as I sit here at my desk this Saturday morning, looking out over Plymouth Sound? I am tired, very tired, because I went to bed late and then got up early to pray, and now I wish I hadn't. Or do I? No, I don't. I just wish I'd gone to bed earlier and slept better. Somewhere, in this personal struggle and chaos lies the reason for my assent to Oliver's request: I wanted to know more about the Apostolic Fathers because I am fascinated by the people of the early Church and because I long to understand more about their search for the unseen God.

Oliver Davies and I lead very different lives, he as a scholar in the heart of Wales and I as a rather driven doctor in a hospice for the terminally ill. So what do we have in common? To put it at its simplest, I suppose, it's God, or rather, a shared hunger for the divine and a common interest in the way ideas of God have developed over the centuries. As an academic, Oliver has the background in philosophy and spirituality which I lack. He knows about Plato, Philo, Gregory of Nyssa, Dionysius and Meister Eckhart and all the key people in the development of Christian spirituality whom I struggle so hard to understand. But why, you might very reasonably ask, do I bother? Why don't I just stick to my medical journals and whodunits and leave the theologians to their erudition and their speculations? The trouble is, I can't stop bothering. I find myself drawn like a bear to the honey pot because the deeper I engage in my work with dying people, the more I find I need to understand about God.

Men and women facing death ask questions, awkward questions, like "Why me? How could God do this to me? How can there be a God if he allows such suffering?" A woman has just died at the hospice. She was riddled with cancer, her face swollen and blue, fighting for breath. Now she is dead and I'm glad for her. But what about her husband, who sits there weeping? What about the nurse who has just said to me, "It's cruel, isn't it? There's no justice, is there?" What am I to say to these people? Am I to tell them that Jesus loves them? Alas, pastoral care is not quite as straightforward as that. *I* know that Jesus loves them, that God is good, and just and infinitely loving, but I must choose my words carefully with people who are desolate and angry. Words may help, of course, but infinitely more powerful than words will be the way my own faith shapes my life and the manner in which I behave toward others.

The nearer that I come to being able to make my own that outrageous claim of St. Paul, "I have been crucified with Christ, and I live now not with my own life but with the life of Christ who lives in me" (Gal 2:20), the clearer they will hear the Good News. And the Good News is worth hearing because it tells us that which we all long to hear: that we are loved.

My question, in the pastoral care of my dying patients is, therefore, not so much how I can persuade them that God loves them, but how can I reveal him to them so that they will *know* that he loves them? Where will I find that living water of which Jesus speaks in his conversation with the woman at the well:

Whoever drinks this water
will get thirsty again;
but anyone who drinks the water that I shall give
will never be thirsty again;
the water that I shall give
will turn into a spring inside him,
welling up to eternal life.

John 4:13

I am a woman, therefore, in search of water, the water of eternal life. My motivation is not in fact as pragmatic as I make out: I am not searching for God because I think it will help my patients but because I personally am thirsty. I have seen a damp patch on the sand, and I am scrambling like a mad thing in the earth in search of living water. David was not just writing a pretty hymn when he wrote Psalm 62. He was voicing that unborn hunger and thirst for God which lie buried in the heart of every human person:

O God you are my God, for you I long,
for you my soul is thirsting.
My body pines for you
like a dry weary land without water.

Psalm 62

There is a passage in the Roman Breviary which reads, "Walk in the dark ways of faith and you will attain the vision of God." I do not know the author of this phrase, only that it is contained in the Office of Readings for Wednesday of the thirty-third week of the year and that it follows a reading from St. Augustine. What I do know, however, is that the words excite me, for I too walk the dark ways of faith in the hope of seeing the unseen God. For me, that search has drawn me not only deeper into my own calling of working with the dying but also back to the roots of my faith as a Christian and, indeed, way back beyond the time of Christ to those people and events that shaped Christianity as we know it today.

It is difficult to convey just how important this journey into the past has been and is to me. As a medical student elect I was channeled early into science and had not even a taste of the classical education that underpins the knowledge and understanding of most of my theologian friends. I knew nothing of the development of Greek civilizations, of the conquest of the Mediterranean by Alexander the Great and the subsequent hellenization of those lands. No one ever tried to teach me philosophy so I knew nothing of the influence of Plato on the Greek concept of God and even less of the way platonic and neoplatonic thought shaped Christianity as we know it today. Like so many Catholic children, I was raised mainly on the gospel stories and shown pictures of a tall man with long hair and a white robe driving the money-lenders out of the temple or being nice to doe-eyed children. I suspect the only reason I didn't ditch the religion of my childhood when I came to university was that Oxford was full of attractive and exciting people who still believed in Christianity and I wanted to belong with them. The other reason that I hung on as a Christian was that I prayed. I prayed out of instinct, out of habit, and because the Catholic chaplain, whom I adored, prayed each morning in the chapel. I prayed, with few words, to a God I could neither imagine nor understand; I prayed not *for* things but simply because God existed. I sat in the dark and wriggled, sometimes bored out of my mind, but sometimes, somehow in touch with something more important than anything else in my life.

All that was more than thirty years ago, and I still sit in

the dark and pray to that which I can neither imagine nor understand. But now I am more knowledgeable and more articulate about it. I know that men and women have had this longing for what I call God since time began and that they have struggled over the years to understand it. I know too that some people are primarily aware of the *transcendence* of God, that he is not like anything or any person we have ever met—that he is totally "other." The Greek philosophers, reacting in disgust against the debauchery of the pantheon of their all too human gods, grappled with the nature of the divine, and became deeply convinced of the "otherness" of God. At first their concept of God was so abstract that they had no sense of a personal Deity who cared for his people. Plato's God was not a God who loved anyone. Later, however, as Greek and Jewish cultures influenced each other, philosophers began to get a sense that this same unknown, transcendent God of Plato was not only immanent, pervading the world, but also entered into relationships with human beings; in other words, he was a *personal* God.

The Hebrew people, of course, had known about the personal nature of the transcendent God for centuries. Such had been their experience of Yahweh in the wilderness that they knew him as father, as friend and as lover. They spoke to him, argued with him, and even wrote love songs to him. They knew quite clearly that he was there in their midst, that he was their God and that they were his people.

In the hellenizing of the Eastern Mediterranean, therefore, we have the gradual coming together of two ideas of God: God as unknowable, as totally other, and God amongst us, travelling with his people and passionately concerned about their welfare and behavior. It has taken

11

me a long time to arrive this far in understanding the development of the idea of God. That which is obvious to those with a classical and philosophical background has come to me with the quality of a revelation.

All at once I see the possibility of integrating my own experience of the mysteriousness of God in prayer with the teaching of my childhood on the incarnation. Having rejected the Jesus of the biblical cinema epics and the Sunday school picture books as a cardboard cut-out, I now find myself posing a question I have never been moved to ask before: what was Jesus of Nazareth like? What sort of a world did he inhabit, and what did the people think about him in those first fifty or one hundred years after his death? Now, when I am not tending my patients, preparing medical lectures or watching police dramas on television, I pore over my atlas of the ancient world and read about Alexander the Great, the Greek philosophers and the early Church Fathers. Like a child with a complicated jigsaw puzzle I piece the story together, searching for the missing pieces which will complete the picture and transform isolated facts into a pattern that I can understand.

The Apostolic Fathers and their writings are a key part of this jigsaw because they form the link between the men who knew Jesus and the later scholars who began to lay down the foundations upon which the edifice of Christian doctrine was constructed. These men knew the people who knew Jesus. Polycarp of Smyrna knew St. John the beloved disciple. I find this fact mind-blowing. I want to shake Polycarp till his old teeth rattle and say, "What did John tell you about Jesus? What was he *like,* for heaven's sake? But, of course, he doesn't tell us. All we get are two letters exhorting the Christians of Philippi to persevere unceasingly in their hope, Jesus Christ.

12

Dry bones. That's all we have: the dried up bones of men long since dead. What can ordinary folk hope to gain from poring over those fragments of letters, and sermons written to men and women of a different time, a different culture, a different race? That's what I thought, a year or so ago until I began this journey back to the roots of Christianity; then, little by little, the dry bones have, like those in Ezekiel's valley, become clothed in flesh. I am reminded of Stanley Spencer's entrancing pictures of the resurrection, men and women emerging, yawning from the grave, wiping the sleep out of their eyes and combing their hair in the morning sunshine.

This is what my encounter with patristics has done for me: the dry bones are becoming clothed in flesh and I begin to know them as people. The man I love most is Ignatius, bishop of Antioch in Syria who walked over a thousand miles to Rome to be martyred, changing the lives of those he met along the way. Ignatius, it seems, followed Euodius, successor of St. Peter as bishop of Antioch in the year AD 69, thirty-six years after the death of Jesus. Of his pastoral life we know nothing save that he struggled to hold his adolescent Christian Church together in a cosmopolitan Middle Eastern city of half a million turbulent people. His flock, it seems, was no less turbulent than their Jewish or pagan contemporaries, and this early Church was in constant peril of being torn apart by internal rivalries and dissensions. Ignatius is a firm disciplinarian and upholder of episcopal authority: and no wonder, for he was protecting a new and vulnerable organization. More fascinating by far, however, than the political storms of the early Church is the man Ignatius became. In the year 107, when he must surely have been well into his sixties or seventies, Ignatius was arrested and sentenced by the provincial magistrates at

Antioch and sent to Rome in chains to be thrown to the wild beasts in the arena.

We can plot his journey to Rome by the letters he wrote along the way, for when the prisoners and their captors stopped to rest, Ignatius met with local Christians and gave them counsel and encouragement. His journey clearly caused a stir, for people came from towns forty or fifty miles away to see this extraordinary man who spoke of his impending death like a lover awaiting a meeting with his beloved: "The limits of the earth and the kingdoms of the world are worth nothing to me. It is better for me to die in Christ than to rule over the ends of the earth. My quest is for him who died for our sake, my desire is for him who rose again for us" (Ignatius' letter to the Romans).

Again and again, if we have ears to listen for it, there comes in spiritual literature this unashamed language of desire. We find it especially in the psalms, and in the prophets, particularly Hosea and Isaiah. God is likened to a faithful spouse, journeying out into the wilderness in search of his errant wife, and taking her back, bruised and defiled to begin their life once more.

> "Do not be afraid, you will not be put to shame," he whispers: "you will not be disgraced. For now your Creator will be your husband. . . . For the mountains may depart, the hills be shaken, but my love for you will never leave you."
>
> *Isaiah 54*

It's powerful stuff, isn't it? Why then, I wonder, should we be surprised to hear the same extravagant language on the lips of religious men and women? They know in their guts that to which we pay only lip service: that

14

God's love is better than life itself and that death is the gateway to real life.

One of the people Ignatius met was Polycarp of Smyrna, who became bishop of that ancient coastal town which was not far from Ephesus where St. John the Apostle lived. John had settled there when numbers of the Church leaders had left the Holy Land prior to the fall of Jerusalem in AD 70. That, we are told, is how Polycarp knew John; and as a disciple he must have grown up imbued with the Johannine message that God is love and those who profess to love God must live out that faith in love of neighbor.

What then must have been the effect upon Polycarp of his meeting with Ignatius when the older bishop was on his way to his death in the Roman arena? Polycarp would have been around thirty-seven at the time he met Ignatius and we know that for the next forty years he kept the letter Ignatius wrote to him. "Cherish unity," Ignatius urged him; "devote yourself to prayers without end." What long hours did Polycarp spend before God in prayer, I wonder, over the ensuing years? Alas, we do not know except that, as an old man in his eighties he went quietly to his own martyrdom, on 23 February just over 120 years after Jesus the Nazarene died on a cross outside Jerusalem.

The Apostolic Fathers, then, were men for whom the legacy of the personal impact of Jesus was very much alive. They were men of the world: bishops and administrators, burdened as bishops always are with wayward priests and squabbling parishioners, deviant scholars and importunate widows. But they weren't just Church administrators, nor indeed just good pastors, they were men in whom the fire of the love of God had taken such an unquenchable hold that they went joyfully to their deaths: truly, to the Jews a stumbling block and to the pagans madness.

And we who have our faith so cushy, what can we do but marvel and beg that a spark from their fire may fly out and set us alight?

Sheila Cassidy

A Note on the Apostolic Fathers

The group of authors known as the "Apostolic Fathers," whose work is contained in this anthology, represents some of the earliest writers of the Christian Church. Some of their work is even contemporary with the canonical writings of the New Testament itself. They represent a stage when Christianity was still detaching itself from its Jewish roots, and these writings offer us a precious glimpse into the realities of the Christian life and vocation at a period when theology and the Church had not yet taken on the fixed form that these would have for later generations. Indeed, one of the finest aspects of these writings is their infectious sense of Christianity as a new and radical religion that demanded of its adherents a full-blooded commitment to faith in Christ and a life founded on his precepts. Although these Fathers are of great historical importance from the point of view of how they understand the sacraments, the teachings and hierarchical structure of the early Church, we have selected passages here which also reflect something of their *discovery* of Christ and his way, and the sense of new life that this gave.

The *Didache* or "Teachings of the Twelve Apostles" is a work that sets out instruction on the meaning and practice of baptism and of the eucharist. It also presents the moral choice confronting the Christian in the form of the Way of Life and the Way of Death. This goes back to an earlier document, which survives independently, and which appears again in the Letter of Barnabas. We know nothing at all about the author of the *Didache*, although the influence of Jewish Christian experience can be felt throughout his work. A Greek-speaking area of Syria has been suggested as the most likely place of origin, and the work must have been written before the middle of the second century.

We can guess that the author of the *Letter of Barnabas,* on the other hand, was an itinerant Christian teacher who may have come from Palestine or Syria. While stressing that the whole of the Old Testament remains relevant to Christians, albeit newly understood, the author of the letter speaks strongly against the judaizers, that is, those who wished to make the new Christian gospel conform to its Jewish origins. It is possible even that the letter belongs to the period shortly after AD 70 and that the author is the same Barnabas who fell out with St. Paul in about AD 50 on account of his own judaizing tendencies (Gal 2:13).

The *Shepherd* can probably be dated to around the year 70 AD and was addressed to the Church in Rome. It is a highly unusual work with its mixture of vision, catechetical instruction and ethical teachings. Although the author, Hermas, tells us a certain amount about himself and his sexual temptations, we do not know how much is autobiographical and how much is symbolic, signifying his attraction perhaps to pagan religion. The sections included here are all taken from the Commandments, the third section of the work, and concern the need for purity of heart and uprightness of life, based upon a belief in the oneness of God who created all things.

In his first letter, *Clement of Rome* presents a vision of a Church unified within its apostolic structures, although he is also well aware of the humility and repentance which are required on all sides if such unity is to be maintained. It was written probably in the last decade of the first century to the community at Corinth, who seem to have been particularly afflicted with strife, by the Clement who was the third bishop of Rome.

The second letter traditionally attributed to this important figure is probably not a letter at all and is certainly not by Clement of Rome. The author stresses above all the role of repentance in the Christian life, and it is through prayer, fasting and charitable giving that we are made whole again. The letter possibly belongs to the early second century.

The Letters of *Ignatius of Antioch* are the remarkable journal of a churchman who was being taken from Antioch to Rome in order to face the wild beasts on account of his faith. The most likely date for this event is during the reign of Trajan, that is between the year 98 and 117. They provide us with insight into a mind that was intent upon sacrifice of the flesh and upon life in the next world. Ignatius was the bishop of Syria, and he may well have been betrayed to the authorities by the disaffected Christians in his own Church. Certainly he lays great stress upon the unity of the Church as well as upon the necessity of following Christ in the way of suffering in order to inherit eternal life. Ignatius wrote letters to a series of churches which came out to greet him on his journey to Rome, and it is these that Polycarp later gathered into a collection.

Polycarp too faced martyrdom at the end of his long life. Born around 69, he was martyred probably in 155. As a young man he had known the apostle John and "others who had seen the Lord," and so Polycarp forms a bridge between these early Christian writings and the apostolic age itself.

The *Letter to Diognetus* is a fine example of Christian apology, which may however belong to a later period than the other works included in this anthology. Nevertheless, it breathes the air of a simple, powerful and primitive Christianity. We are certain neither of the identity of the author nor of the recipient, but whoever the author was, he writes magnificently of the truly supernatural nature of the Christian life.

Oliver Davies

The Didache

The Two Ways

There are two ways, one of life and one of death, and there is a great difference between them. The way of life is this: "First of all, you are to love the God who made you. Secondly, you are to love your neighbor as yourself. And do not do to another what you would not have done to yourself."

Now the teaching of these words is this: "Bless those who curse you and pray for your enemies, and fast for those who persecute you. What credit is it to you if you love those who love you? Do not even the heathen do as much? But, for your part, love those who hate you and you will have no enemy."

Abstain from carnal and bodily appetites. If someone strikes you on the right cheek, then offer them the other as well, and you will be perfect. If someone compels you to go one mile, then go two miles with them. If someone wants to steal your coat from you, then give them your shirt as well. If someone wants to take from you what is yours, do not demand it back. Give to everyone who asks of you, and do not refuse them, for the Father wishes that we should give to all from what we have ourselves received.

Happy are they who give according to the commandment, for they are innocent. But woe to those who receive. If it is from their need, then they are innocent, but they who receive without need shall be tried as to why they took it and for what purpose. Held in prison they shall be examined as to what they have done, and they shall not get out of that place until they have paid the last penny. But there is a saying about this too: "Let your alms sweat in your hands until you know to whom you are giving."

(1)

The Way of Life — I

My child, keep clear of every evil person and all who are like them. Do not be quick-tempered, since anger leads to murder. And do not be jealous, or argumentative, or get too heated about things, for all these lead to murder.

My child, keep away from lust, because lust leads to sins of impurity. Do not use obscene words, or let your eyes wander, for all these things lead to adultery.

Do not peer into omens, my child, since this leads to idolatry. Do not be an enchanter, an astrologer, a magician, or even wish to explore these things, for they all lead to idolatry.

My child, do not tell lies, for lying leads to theft. Do not be boastful or too fond of money, for all these things lead to theft.

Do not grumble, my child, for this leads to blasphemy, and do not be stubborn or think evil, for all these things lead to blasphemy.

Be meek rather, for the meek shall inherit the earth. Be patient, merciful, innocent, quiet, good and full of respect for the words you have heard. Do not exalt yourself or become arrogant. Do not associate with the high and mighty, but keep the company of those who are honest and humble.

Accept that what befalls you is good in the knowledge that nothing happens without God.

(3)

The Way of Life — II

My child, remember day and night the one who speaks the Word of God to you and honor him as you would the Lord, for where the nature of the Lord is spoken of, there the Lord is. Seek out the faces of God's holy people every day, because their words will bring rest to your soul. Do not desire to break away, but pacify the warring factions. Judge fairly, without favoring any one person when searching out crimes. Do not hover between two minds as to whether something is to be or not.

You must not be the sort of person who stretches out their hands to receive but keeps them closed when it comes to giving. You will give a ransom for your sins from what you have earned by your hands. Do not hesitate to give, and do not grumble as you are giving. You should know who is the good paymaster of the reward. Do not turn the needy away, but share everything with your brothers and sisters, and do not say that it is your own. If you are sharers together in what will never pass away, how much more in things that will soon perish?

Do not spoil your son or daughter, but teach them the fear of God from their youth up. Do not turn your wrath against your servant or your maid, who have their hope in the same God as you, in case they should cease to fear the God who is over you both. God does not come to call us with any respect for persons but calls those who have been prepared by the Spirit. . . .

You should loathe all hypocrisy, and anything else which the Lord finds displeasing. You are not to neglect the Lord's commands but faithfully keep what you have received, "not adding to it or taking anything away." Own up to your sins and failings in the assembly and avoid coming to your prayer with a bad conscience. This is the way of life.

(4)

The Eucharist: How to Give Thanks

As regards the eucharist of thanksgiving, this is how you should give thanks.

Over the cup first of all: "We give thanks to you our Father, for the Holy Vine of David, your child, which you made known to us through your child, Jesus. Yours be the glory for ever more." Then over the bread that is broken: "We give thanks to you, our Father, for the life and the true knowledge which you have made known to us through Jesus, your child. Yours be the glory for ever more. As this broken bread was scattered over the hills and was brought together and made into one, so may your Church be gathered together from the ends of the earth into your kingdom. Yours indeed is the glory and the power through Jesus Christ for ever."

But no one is to eat or drink of our eucharist other than those who have been baptized in the name of the Lord. The Lord himself has already spoken about this: "Do not give that which is holy to the dogs."

(9)

The Eucharist: Prayer of Thanksgiving

When you have satisfied your need, give thanks in this way: "We thank you, holy Father, for your holy name which you have caused to dwell in our hearts and for the knowledge and faith and immortality which you have made known to us through Christ, your child. Yours is the glory, throughout all ages. You, Almighty Master, created all things for your name's sake. You gave food and drink to the human race for its enjoyment so that it should give you thanks. But to us you have given spiritual food and drink and life eternal through your child. Above all we give thanks to you for your power. Yours is the glory for ever. Remember, Lord, your Church. Guard it from evil and perfect it in your love. Gather her together from the four winds and bring her, purified and sanctified, into your kingdom which you have prepared for her. Yours, O Lord, is the power and the glory for ever and ever. Let grace come and let this world pass away. Hosannah to the God of David. If anyone is holy, let them come. If they are not, let them repent. Maranatha. Amen."

But let the prophets conduct the eucharist as they will.

(10)

The Eucharist: How to Approach It

On Sunday, the Lord's day, break bread and give your eucharistic thanks and praise, having first confessed your sins and failings so that your offering may be pure. But anyone who has a quarrel with another is not to join with you until they have made peace, otherwise your sacrifice will be defiled. Listen to the Lord's own words: "In every place, at every time, offer me a pure sacrifice, because I am a great king, says the Lord, and my name is held in awe among all the nations."

(4)

The Letter of Barnabas

Spiritual Counsel

We ought to inquire carefully into the things that are upon us at present, seeking out those that can contribute toward our salvation. We should keep well clear of the works of lawlessness in case they may overwhelm us. We should hate the errors of the day so that we may be loved in what is to come. We should not give our souls the freedom to mix with sinners and those who are evil or we may become like them. . . .

Let us be alert then in these last days, for the whole of our life in the faith will be worth nothing unless we stand firm, as befits the children of God, in this present evil time and in the trials to come so that the evil one may find no way in. We should shun all vanity, despising the acts that belong to the path of evil. Do not live apart, as if you were already perfect, but join with others and seek out the common good. Scripture says: "How pitiful are those who think they have understanding, and are wise in their own eyes." Let us be spiritual people, a temple fit for God. Let us train ourselves as far as we can in the fear of God, and try hard to keep his commandments so that we delight in his ordinances.

The Lord will have no partiality when he comes to judge the world. Each will receive as each has done. If someone is good, their goodness will go before them. If they are wicked, then the reward of their wickedness will stand before them. This should prevent us from resting on our laurels as though we were called, and from slumbering in our sins, so that the evil one can gain power over us and in the end drive us out from the Lord's kingdom. Remember this, my brothers and sisters, when you consider the number and power of the signs and wonders which were done in Israel, that still they were abandoned. Therefore we must take great care that what was written becomes true of us, that "many are called but few are chosen."

(4)

Spiritual Meditation

Keep the company of those who fear the Lord, those who ponder in their hearts the meaning of the word they have received, those who speak of and keep the Lord's instructions, those who know that meditation is a work of gladness and who deliberate on the work of the Lord.

(10)

The Temple of God

Is there such a thing as a temple of God? Yes, there is, for he himself says that he makes it and perfects it. It is written: "It will happen that when the week is ended the temple of God will be built gloriously in the name of the Lord." So I find that a temple does exist.

This is how it shall be built in the name of the Lord. Before we came to believe in the Lord, the habitation of our own heart was corrupt and weak like a temple which has really been built by human hands, because it was full of idolatry and was a house of demons through the doing of those things which are against God. But "it will be built in the name of the Lord."

Now pay close attention: so that the Lord's temple may indeed be built gloriously, learn exactly how it is built. When we received the remission of our sins and placed our hope in the sacred name of God, we became entirely new and were created again from the beginning. So it is that God now dwells in us in truth, in this habitation that we ourselves are. But by what means? His word of faith, the call of his promise, the wisdom of his statutes, the commands of his teaching, himself prophesying within us, himself dwelling in us, by opening the door of the temple, which is to say the mouth, giving us repentance and leading us, who have been enslaved in death, into the incorruptible temple.

They who desire to be saved do not look at the individual but at the one who dwells and speaks within the individual. And they are amazed, for they have never heard that person speak such words before nor have they themselves ever wished to hear them. This then is the spiritual temple which is being built for the Lord.

(16)

The Way of Light

We must now move on to another lesson and teaching. There are two ways of teaching and power: the way of light and the way of darkness. And there is a great deal of difference between these two ways. Over the one are set the light-bearing angels of God, while over the other are posted the angels of Satan. The one is Lord from eternity to eternity, and the other is the ruler of the present age of wrong-doing.

Now the way of light is as follows, and if anyone desires to make their way to the appointed place, then they should be industrious in their works. The knowledge which has been given to us of how we are to walk this way is this:

You are to love the One who made you, you are to fear the One who fashioned you, you are to give glory to the One who redeemed you from death. You are to be of a single heart and rich in spirit. You are not to join company with those who walk the path of death. Everything that is displeasing to God you are to hate, as you are to hate all hypocrisy. Do not abandon the Lord's commands. Do not exalt yourself, but show humility in all things. Do not take glory for yourself. Never form an evil plan against your neighbor, and do not let your soul grow arrogant. You are not to commit acts of unchastity or adultery or to corrupt boys. The word of God must not depart from you even amidst the impurity of others. Never show partiality when it comes to reproving someone for their misdeeds. Be meek, be gentle and quiet; receive the words you hear with awe. Do not bear ill-will toward your brother or sister. Do not hover between two minds as to whether something is to be or not. You must not take the Lord's name in vain, and you must love your neighbor more than you love your own life. Do not procure abortion, nor kill new-born children. Do not spoil your son or daughter, but rather instruct them in the fear of the Lord from their youth up. You are not to desire your neighbor's possessions, nor to be grasping. You should not cling in your soul to the high and mighty, but rather keep the company of those who are humble and good. Receive the various events which befall you as good, in the knowledge that nothing happens without God. Do not be fickle or a gossip. Be subject to your masters in reverence and fear as those who represent God for you. Do not give harsh orders to your maid or servant, who hope in the same God, in case they should lose their reverence for the God who is above you both and who did not come to call us with any respect to persons but called those whom the spirit had prepared. Share everything with your neighbor, without saying that things are your own. If you are sharers together in things that will never pass away, then how much more so in things that will soon disappear. Do not be too quick to speak, for your mouth is a death-snare. And as far as you possibly can, keep your soul pure.

Do not be the type who stretches out their hands to receive but closes them tightly when it comes to giving. Love the person who speaks the word of the Lord to you as the apple of your eye. Remember the Day of Judgement day and night, and seek out every day the faces of God's holy people, either laboring in speech by exhorting others and trying to save souls by what you say, or by working with your hands for the remission of your sins. Do not be slow to give and do not grumble as you are giving, but know who is the good paymaster of the reward. Keep faithfully what you have received, neither adding to it nor taking anything away.

Hate evil utterly. Judge rightly. Do not cause quarrels, but bring together and reconcile those who have fallen out. Confess your sins. Do not come to prayer with a bad conscience. This is the way of light.

(18, 19)

Be Faithful

So it is good that they who have learnt as many of the Lord's ordinances as have been put into writing should walk in them. For they who put them into practice shall be glorified in the kingdom of God, while those who choose the alternative will pass into the same perdition as their works. This is why there is a resurrection; this is why there is a reward. Those of you who are in high positions, if you are willing to take my well-meaning advice, I have an earnest request to make of you. Keep amongst yourselves people to whom you may do good; do not fail in this. The day is near when all things shall perish with the evil one. The Lord is near and his reward with him. I beg and implore you, be good lawgivers to one another; be faithful counsellors to one another and remove every kind of hypocrisy from your midst.

And now may God, who is Lord of the whole world, give you wisdom, understanding, discernment, knowledge of what his will has ordained, and endurance. Let God be your teacher, as you seek out what the Lord requires of you, and see that you are found faithful in the Day of Judgement. If there are any memories of the good, then meditate on these things and think once again of me so that my anxious concern and sleepless nights shall not have been in vain. I ask this of you, of your favor. While the fair vessel that holds your soul is yet unbroken, see that you do not fail in any of these things, but pursue them diligently and fulfil every commandment. They are indeed important matters. And so it is that I have been all the more concerned to write to you to the very best of my ability, to give you cause for joy.

Children of love, children of peace, salvation can now be yours. The Lord of glory and of all grace be with your spirit.

(21)

The Shepherd

The Angel of Repentance

When I was praying at home and sitting on my bed, a man entered who was glorious to look upon, dressed like a shepherd and covered with a white goat's skin, carrying a bag on his shoulder and a staff in his hand. He greeted me and I returned his greeting. Immediately he sat at my side and said: "I have been sent by the most holy angel to dwell with you for all the days of your life that are left you." I thought that he had come to tempt me and I said to him: "Who are you? For I know," I said, "to whom I have been handed over." He replied: "Do you not recognize me?" "I do not." He said: "I am the shepherd to whom you were handed over." Even while he spoke, his appearance changed and I recognized him, seeing that he was the one to whom I had been handed over. I was immediately seized by fear and was mortified that I had answered him so rudely and stupidly. But he answered me, saying: "Don't be shocked, but be firm in the commandments which I am going to give you. For I have been sent," he said, "to show you again all those things which you saw before, for these are the chief points which are of help to you. First of all, write down my commandments and parables, but you should also write down the other things as I show you. . . ."

So I wrote down the commandments and parables as he told me to. If then you listen to them and keep them and walk in them and carry them out with a pure heart, you shall receive from the Lord all that he has promised you. If you listen to them and do not repent, but continue in your sin, then you shall receive the opposite from your

Lord. The shepherd, who is the angel of repentance, commanded me to write down all these things.

First Commandment

First of all, you should believe that God is one, who made all things and perfected them, who brought all things into being from that which was not and who contains all things without himself being contained. You should believe in him and should fear him and, through fear of him, you should live a disciplined life. If you keep these things, then you shall throw off all evil and shall clothe yourself in every virtue of righteousness and shall live for God, if you keep this commandment.

Second Commandment

The shepherd said to me: "Be simple and innocent, and you shall be like the children who do not know the evil that destroys the life of men and women."

"Firstly, do not slander anyone, and do not listen willingly to those who speak evil of others in case you share in their sin by listening to them if you believe the slander that you hear. For if you believe such things, then you too will have something against your brother or sister, and will share in the sin of the slanderer. Speaking evil of people is wicked. It is a restless demon that never makes peace but always lives in conflict. Give slander a wide berth then and you will have good relationships with all."

"Clothe yourself in holiness, which contains no stumbling-block of evil but in which all is smooth and joyful. Do good, and from the labors that God gives you, give generously to those who are in need, not vacillating as to whom you shall or shall not give. Give to all, for God wishes all to receive from his own gifts."

Fifth Commandment

"**B**e patient," the shepherd said, "and wise, and then you will have mastery over all the works of evil and you will perform all righteousness. If you are patient, then the Holy Spirit who dwells in you will be pure and will not be eclipsed by any other evil spirit but shall have space to live, rejoicing and delighting with the body in which it dwells, and will serve God with great cheerfulness, possessing well-being in itself."

"But if any irritability enters in, then the Holy Spirit, which is delicate, will immediately be pushed aside, not having a pure place in which to be, and will try to depart from there. It will be choked by the evil spirit, lacking space to serve God as it desires, and is tainted by bad temper."

"For the Lord dwells in patience and the devil in bad temper. If both spirits coexist, then it is harmful and evil for the person concerned. For if you take a tiny bit of wormwood and put it into a jar of honey, will not the whole of the honey be spoilt? A great quantity of honey will be spoilt by a tiny bit of wormwood, so that the sweetness of the honey is lost and it is no longer as pleasing to its owner, since it has been mixed and made useless. But if no wormwood is put into the honey, the honey is found to be sweet and is useful to its owner. You can see that patience is very sweet, more so than honey, and is of great value to the Lord, and he dwells within it. But bad temper is bitter and useless."

Tenth Commandment

"Clothe yourself in joy, which always finds favor with God and is acceptable to him, and blossom in it. Joyful people do good deeds, think good thoughts and spurn sorrow, while those who are sorrowful do evil."

"They do evil, firstly, because they grieve the Holy Spirit which is given us in joy and, secondly, they grieve the Holy Spirit by doing lawless things, by not praying or praising the Lord. The prayers of the sorrowful always lack the power to ascend to the altar of the Lord."

"Why do the prayers of the sorrowful not ascend to the altar?" I asked.

"Because sorrow sits in their hearts," the shepherd replied. "Accordingly the sorrow which is mixed with his prayer does not allow it to ascend in purity to the altar. Just as wine mixed with vinegar is not as pleasant, sorrow limits the power of the Holy Spirit to pray in us. Therefore, purify yourself of this evil sorrow, and you shall live to God, and all shall live to God who shed this sorrow and clothe themselves in joy."

Twelfth Commandment

"**B**ut I, the angel of repentance, say to you: do not fear the devil, for I was sent to be with you who repent with all your heart, to strengthen you in the faith. Believe in God therefore, though you have despaired of your lives on account of your sins and have added to your sins and have made your lives heavy with sin. Believe that if you turn to the Lord with all your heart and perform righteousness for all the days of your life and serve him uprightly according to his will, he will heal your former sins and you shall have the power to master the works of the devil. Do not be afraid of the devil's threat, for he is as powerless as the sinews of a dead man. Listen to me, then, and fear the one who has all power to save and to destroy. If you keep these commandments, then you shall live to God."

I said to him: "Sir, now I have been empowered in all the requirements of the Lord because you are with me. I know that you will destroy all the power of the devil and we shall master him and shall be victorious over all his works. And I hope, Sir, that I shall now be able to keep these commandments which you have given, if the Lord gives me strength."

"You shall keep them," he said, "if your heart is pure toward the Lord, and all those who purify their hearts from the empty desires of this world shall keep them and shall live to God."

Clement's First Letter
to the Corinthians

The Glorious Rule of Tradition

Our purpose in writing this to you is not just to give you good advice but also to stir our own memory, for we are in the same arena and are faced with the same struggle. It is for this reason that we must lay aside empty cares and problems and come at once to the glorious and venerable rule of our tradition. We have to look carefully at what our Maker finds good and pleasing and at those things which are acceptable in his eyes. Let us fix our gaze on the blood of Christ and be fully aware how precious it is to the Father, because it was poured out to set us free and it brought the grace of repentance to the entire world.

Let us consider all the generations and see for ourselves that in one generation after another the Master has given a place of repentance to any who are willing to return to him. Noah preached a change of heart, and those who followed him were saved. Jonah forewarned the Ninevites of the impending disaster, who, when they repented, obtained forgiveness for their sins in answer to their prayer, even though they were strangers to God.

The ministers of God's grace spoke about repentance through the Holy Spirit, and even the Lord of the universe himself spoke of it in the form of an oath: "For as I live," says the Lord, "I do not desire the death of a sinner so much as his repentance."

(7)

Humility of Spirit

So we must be of humble mind, dear brothers and sisters, and shed anything that smacks of arrogance, conceit, stupidity or rage. We must practice what is written, for the Holy Spirit says: "Let not the wise man boast of his wisdom, nor the strong man of his strength, nor the rich man of his riches, but if anyone would boast, let his boast be in the Lord, as he seeks him out and performs acts of justice and righteousness."

We should bear in mind especially the words of the Lord Jesus, which he spoke when he was teaching gentleness and patient endurance. This was his message: "Be merciful and you will obtain mercy. Forgive and you will be forgiven. As you do to others, so it will be done to you. As you give, so will you be given to. As you judge, so will you be judged. As you are kind, so will kindness be shown to you. The measure you give will be the measure you get."

With this commandment and these directives to guide us, let us resolve to walk in obedience to his sacred words and in humility of spirit. For, as the divine word reminds us: "On whom shall I look, but on the meek, the quiet, the one who trembles at my word?"

(13)

Hasten to God

The humility and submissive obedience of so many well-known Old Testament figures has not only done us good, but it also improved the generations that went before us, who received the Lord's oracles in fear and truth. But now that we have received a share in many great deeds of glory, we must hasten on to that goal of peace which was set before us at the beginning, with our eyes fixed on the Father, the Creator of the whole universe, and hold to the magnificent gifts of peace which he has lavished upon us.

With our mind we should contemplate him, and with the eyes of our soul we should gaze hard on his purpose which displays such great patience. And let us recognize how free from anger God is toward all his creatures.

The heavens, which move at his command, are subject to him in peace. Day and night follow the course that he himself allotted them without confusion. The sun, the moon and the choirs of stars all proceed in accordance to his command. With one mind they exactly follow the path marked out for them, and do not swerve from it. The teeming earth brings forth fruit in the proper season according to his will, yielding nourishment in full abundance for human beings and beasts and for all creatures, without dissenting from or changing any of his decrees. Those parts of the depths which no one has ever plumbed and the unexplored regions of the underworld are all under the control of the same supreme command. The hollow of the endless sea is gathered by his divine action into the places allotted to it and it does not cross the barriers set around it, but follows his command. For he said: "You will come thus far, and your waves will break within you." The ocean, untraversed by human-kind, together with the worlds beyond it, are ruled by the same masterful directives. The seasons of spring, summer, autumn and winter give place to one another peacefully. The winds play their roles at the proper time. And the ever-flowing springs, which were created for our enjoyment and our health, are unfailing in their sustenance of human life. Even the smallest animals come together in concord and peace.

All these things were commanded by the great Creator and Master of the universe to keep peace and harmony, who does good to all things, and especially to us who have sought refuge in his compassion through our Lord Jesus Christ. To him be glory and majesty for all eternity. Amen.

Take care, my dearest brothers and sisters, lest his many good works for us should become a judgement against us, which they will if we fail to be citizens worthy of him, and if we do not perform fine and excellent works before him with one mind. For in one place he says: "The Spirit of the Lord is a lamp that searches out the most secret parts."

We have only to look to see how close he is and that nothing which goes on in our thinking or intentions ever escapes his notice. It is right, therefore, that we do not desert his will. We would do better to give offence to silly, thoughtless people, who are presumptuous and who get carried away in their proud utterances, than to God.

Let us give our Lord Jesus Christ the reverence that is his due. It was his own blood that was given for us. Let us respect those who govern us and those who are advanced in years. As for the young, we should instruct and educate them in the fear of God. And we should lead our wives to what is good. They should display that beauty and attraction which a pure way of life alone can give, and should show sincerity of purpose in their humility. Let them prove the gentleness of their tongue by their silences. They should not show affection through partiality to only a few, but fairly and nobly to all who fear God. As for our children, let them have a part in the formation which is in Christ and learn the strength of humility before God. Let them grasp what power love has in his sight, how great and how beautiful is the fear of him which gives salvation to all who walk in that spirit in holiness and purity of mind.

For he searches our thoughts and our desires. It is his breath that we have in us, and when he sees fit, he will take it away.

(19, 20, 21)

God's Promises

The good workman receives the bread of his labor boldly, whereas the lazy, careless person hardly dares to look his employer in the face. So we must be prompt in our good works, since all that comes to us is from him. Indeed, he gives us this warning: "Look, the Lord is coming. His reward is before his face. He will pay each according to their work."

And so it is that he exhorts each of us who believe in him with an undivided heart not to be lazy or careless in the good that we do. Our boast, our confidence, ought to be in him, and we should be subject to his will. We need only consider the whole host of angels that surround him, to see how they stand ready, always at the service of his will. As the scripture says: "Ten thousand times ten thousand stood by him, and a thousand thousands were ministering to him, and crying: 'Holy, holy, holy is the Lord of Sabaoth. The whole of creation is full of his glory.' "

And so we too ought to gather together in harmony of conscience, and cry earnestly to him as it were with one mouth, that we may have a share in his great and glorious promises. As he says: "Eye has not seen, nor ear heard, nor human heart conceived what it is that the Lord has prepared for those who wait for him."

(34)

How to Receive God's Gifts

How richly blessed, how wonderful are God's gifts, my dear people? Life in immortality, splendor in righteousness, truth in boldness, faith in confidence, self-control in sanctity—and, what is more, all these things are placed within the grasp of our understanding.

What then are the things that are being prepared for those who wait for him? The Creator and Father of the ages, the all holy One, he himself knows their greatness and beauty. We for our part must strive to be found among the number of those who wait, so that we too may have a share in these promised gifts.

But how, dear people, shall this be? It will come about only if our minds are fixed faithfully on God; if we seek those things that please and satisfy him; if we carry out fully what is in harmony with his will, which cannot err; and if we walk in the way of truth. It will happen if we free ourselves from all evil and wrong-doing, from greed, wrangling, ill-will and deceit, from gossip and back-biting, contempt for God, pride and arrogance, conceit and lack of hospitality. Those who indulge in these things can only be hateful to God, and this is true not only of those who commit these faults but also of those who encourage them.

(35)

Christ, the Way

This is the way, dear people, by which we have found our salvation: Jesus Christ, the high priest of our offerings, the one who supports us and helps us in our weakness. It is through him that we fix our gaze on heaven's heights; through him we see the reflection of God's glorious and most exalted face; through him we receive the blossoming toward the light of our dull and darkened understanding. And it was through him that the Master willed that we should have a taste of that knowledge which will never die.

(36)

The Army of God

For our part then, brothers and sisters, we must serve in our own army with great commitment, obeying every one of its unerring commands.

Let us call to mind those who serve our generals and who obey their commands with such perfect order, promptness and submission. We know that they are not all prefects, tribunes, centurions or even minor officers, yet each and every one of them carries out the orders issued by the sovereign and the generals, according to the rank that they hold. The great can no more exist without the small than can the small without the great. There is a certain interdependence, and this is what makes everything work.

If we consider our body, then we see the same pattern: the head is of no use without the feet—nor the feet, for that matter, without the head. The smallest parts of our body are necessary and valuable for the body as a whole; all work and act together in order to preserve the whole body.

So let our whole body be preserved in Christ Jesus, and let each one of us be subject to our neighbor, according to the position and the function they have been given. The strong should care for the weak, and the weak should respect the strong. The rich should come to the aid of the poor, and the poor should give thanks to God for giving them someone to help them in their need. Those who are wise should show their wisdom in good deeds, rather than in words, and the person of humble mind should not bear witness to their own humility but leave this task to others. Let those who remain pure in the flesh not be boastful, in the knowledge that it is another who gives them their self-control.

So, dear brothers and sisters, let us consider for a moment of what stuff we are made and what our nature was when we came into this world. Let us consider how he who made us and formed us led us out from the darkness of the grave into the world, preparing all kinds of good things for us even before we were born. Since we have all these things from him, we should give thanks to him for everything, to whom be glory for ever and ever. Amen.

(37, 38)

Serving the Common Good

We must quickly put a stop to this conflict and simply fall down before our Master. In tears we should plead with him to look upon us with mercy, to be reconciled to us and to restore us to that noble and holy practice of brotherly love of ours. For this is the gate of righteousness which opens on to life. As scripture puts it: "Open to me the gates of righteousness, that I may enter by them and give thanks to the Lord. This is the Lord's own gate. The righteous will enter by it."

So of the many gates open before us, it is the one of righteousness which is Christ's own gate. They are blessed who enter into it, who walk in the ways of holiness and righteousness and who accomplish all things without fuss. Each of us should be faithful; each should have the power of the initiated to utter "knowledge"; each should be wise in the discernment of truth; and each should be pure in all things done. The greater we seem to be, the more humble we must be, and the more we must seek the common good and not our own.

(48)

Opening the Heart's Eyes to God

Help us to place our hope in your name, O Lord, which is the source of all creation, and to open the eyes of our heart to recognize that you alone are the highest in the highest, the holy One who abides among the holy. It is you who crush the pride of the arrogant and reduce to nothing the plans of the nations. You raise up on high those who are brought low and bring down those who are raised up. You bring riches to some and allow others to go poor. Some you slay, while to others you give new life. You alone are the searcher of spirits and are the God of all flesh. You gaze into the depths and see all that we do. You come to the help of those in danger and save those in despair. You are the Creator of every spirit, and you watch over them all. You have increased the nations over all the earth and from them you have chosen those who love you through Jesus Christ, your beloved Child. Through him you have taught us, you have made us holy and have brought us honor.

(49)

A Blessing

And now may God, who sees all things, who is Master of spirits and Lord of all flesh, and who chose the Lord Jesus Christ and us through him to be his very own people, grant to every soul which has received the invocation of his sublime and holy name, the gifts of faith, fear, peace, patient endurance, self-control, purity and moderation. May we thus be pleasing to his name through our high-priest, the champion of our race, Jesus Christ. For it is through this same Christ that all will receive glory and majesty, might and honor, both now and for all ages to come.

(64)

Clement's Second Letter to the Corinthians

God's Mercy

My brothers and sisters, when we think of Jesus Christ, we must think of him as God, as "judge of the living and the dead." And we must not take our own salvation lightly. Our thinking lightly of him is a sure sign of our hoping little from him. And those who are listening and thinking to themselves "All this matters very little" are sinning even now. And so are we, for that matter, if we have no idea from where we have been called, who called us, and to what place we are called, and if we have forgotten the terrible sufferings that Jesus Christ underwent for our sake.

What, then, shall we give him in return, or what fruit shall we offer that shall be worthy of what he has given us? How great a debt of holiness we owe him! He gave us the light, he called us his "child" as a father does, he saved us when we faced destruction. How, then, shall we praise him or repay him for all that we have received? We were in a state of mental blindness. We worshipped stones and pieces of wood, not to mention gold, silver and copper: the works of human hands. Our whole life was nothing other than death. We were immersed in thick darkness, and mist completely obscured our vision. But we were given back our sight, and it was his will that we should be free of that cloud which surrounded us. He had pity on us, and he saved us in his mercy. What he saw was the great error and destruction which was within us, and that we had no hope of salvation apart from him. For he called us when we were not, and it was his will that we should come to be.

(1)

Detachment from the World

And so, brothers and sisters, let us not be quite so much at home in this world, and let us do the will of him who called us. Nor should we fear leaving this world, for the Lord said: "You will be as lambs in the middle of wolves." Peter's answer was: "And what if the wolves tear the lambs to pieces?" Jesus said to Peter: "The lambs need have no fear of the wolves once they are dead. And you too need not fear those who put you to death, and can do nothing more to you. But the one you need to fear is he who, after taking away your life, has power over your soul and body, and can cast them into hell fire."

Know for certain, my friends, that our abiding in this world in the flesh is a little thing and lasts only a short time, whereas Christ's promise is something great and wonderful. This is the repose of the coming kingdom, of life that has no end.

And so what shall we do to attain these things? We must lead a holy and just life, certainly, and not regard the things of the world as our own, or desire them in any way. For when we set our hearts and minds on these things, we wander from the way of righteousness.

(5)

Commitment

And so, dear friends, let us fight hard, knowing that the struggle is close at hand and that many people make long sea-voyages for the sake of quickly forgotten contests. Not all win crowns, but only those who have made a great effort and have fought well. Let us then fight well, so that we may all be crowned. Let us run the straight course, the immortal contest, and let us go in great numbers to compete that we may also win the crown. And if not all of us can win the crown, then let us at least be close runners-up!

(7)

The Virtue of Repentance

While we are still on earth, let us have a change of heart. We are clay in the hands of the workman. When the potter makes his vessel, he sometimes finds that it bends or breaks in his hands. When this happens, he immediately sets about remodelling it. But he can do nothing more for it once he has put it into the oven and applied heat to it. So too let us grasp our chance while we are in this world. Let us repent wholeheartedly of all the evil we have done in the flesh, so the Lord may save us while we still have time for repentance. Once we have gone from this world, we can never make our confession or change direction again in the place that awaits us there.

So then, my friends, if we have accomplished the Father's will, keeping our fleshly selves pure and following the Lord's commands, we shall obtain eternal life. As the Lord says in the gospel: "If you do not guard something which is small, who will give you something that is really important? I tell you that the one who is faithful in little things is faithful also in great things."

What he is saying is this: Keep the flesh pure and the seal of baptism undefiled, so that we may gain eternal life.

(8)

74

God the Healer

Let none of you say that this flesh is not judged and does not rise again. Discern for yourself: in what state did you receive salvation, in what state did you receive your sight, if not in this flesh? It is our duty to guard the flesh as God's own temple, because as you were called in the flesh, so shall you come to complete salvation in the flesh. If Christ, the Lord who saved us, in fact became flesh even though he was originally spirit, and in this state called us, then we too are to receive our reward in this very same flesh. So let us love one another and thus we shall, each and every one of us, come to God's kingdom.

While there is still time for us to be healed, let us entrust ourselves to the God who makes us whole, giving him his due as a healer. And what is it that we owe him? Repentance from a sincere heart. He has knowledge of every single thing before it happens, and he certainly knows what lies hidden in our hearts. So let us give him praise, not only with our lips, but also with our hearts. In this way he will receive us as his children. The Lord himself said: "My brothers and sisters are those who do the will of my Father."

(9)

The Blasphemy We Provoke

It is high time, my friends, that we had a change of heart and began to be sensible with regard to what is good. The truth is that there is still a good deal of stupidity and wickedness in us. We need to wipe all our former sins completely away. If we repent from the depth of our soul, then we shall be saved. And let us not just seek to please others, or ourselves alone by our right living, but we should please outsiders as well, so that the name of God will not be blasphemed on our account.

For the Lord says: "My name is forever being blasphemed among all the nations." And again: "Woe to those on whose account my name is blasphemed."

But where is the blasphemy? It is in your failing to do what I desire. Whenever the heathen hear the oracles of God from our mouth, they wonder at their beauty and majesty. But then when they come to learn of the way we actually behave and see how far removed our actions are from the words that we say, their wonder turns to blasphemy, and they say that this is a myth and delusion.

For instance, when they hear from us that God says: "It is no credit to you if you love merely those who love you, but it is a credit to you if you love your enemies and those who hate you," then they are quite amazed at this extraordinary goodness. But when they see for themselves that not only do we not love those who hate us, but we do not even love those who love us, then they have a good laugh at us and the name of God is blasphemed.

(13)

The True Church

My friends, if we do the will of God our Father, we shall be part of that first Church, the spiritual one, that was created before the sun and the moon. But if, on the other hand, we do not do the Lord's will, we shall fall under that text of scripture which says: "My house has become a den of thieves." So let us make a conscious choice to belong to the Church of life. This is how we shall be saved. . . .

If we say that the flesh is the Church, and that the Spirit is Christ, then it follows, of course, that whoever has abused the flesh has abused the Church. Such a person will therefore have no share in the Spirit, which is Christ. The very same flesh has the possibility of receiving a tremendous gift of life and incorruption, if the Holy Spirit is joined to it. And no one on earth can express or even speak of the things the Lord has prepared for his chosen ones.

(14)

Encouraging One Another

Let us repent wholeheartedly, that none of us may be lost by the wayside. If we are commanded to go even further than this and rescue souls from idols and give them a proper formation, how much more is it our duty to ensure that a soul that already knows God is not lost? Let us then help one another and bring those who are weak back to a good life.

In this way, we shall all come to salvation and bring one another back to the right path through mutual help and advice. More than that, we should not only seem to believe correctly and seem to take these things seriously while we are being exhorted by our elders, but, even when we have gone home, we should bring to mind the Lord's commandments and not be dragged off course by worldly desires.

On the contrary, let us gather here more often and try to make progress in the commandments the Lord has left us. Thus we shall "all be of one mind" and shall be gathered together into Life.

(17)

A Personal Prayer

Let us too belong among the number of those who give thanks in the eucharist, who have served God and are not counted among the profane people who are to be judged. For I too am altogether sinful and have not yet escaped temptation but am surrounded by the snares of the devil. And yet I struggle to pursue righteousness so that I may be strong enough to draw near to it, in fear of the judgement which is to come.

(18)

Complete Conversion

Therefore, my brothers and sisters, in accord with the God of truth I am reading you an exhortation to pay attention to the scriptures, so that you yourselves and the reader in your midst may be saved. All I ask in return is that you should repent from the bottom of your heart, thus winning yourselves salvation and life. If we do this, we shall be setting a goal for the younger ones who wish to devote themselves to the cause of piety and God's goodness.

And we should not be foolishly irritated and annoyed when someone corrects us and tries to turn us from the wrong to the right path. We sometimes do things that are wrong without being aware of it. This is the result of the inconstancy and lack of faith which lies deep within us. Our minds are indeed darkened by empty desires.

Let us then put our righteousness into practice, so that in the end we may be saved. Those who obey these instructions are blessed. Though they suffer for a short while in this world, they shall gain the immortal fruit of the resurrection. So the devout should not grieve if, for the time being, they seem to have much to endure, for a time of blessedness awaits them. That soul will live again on high with those who have gone before, and its rejoicing will extend to an eternity free of sorrow.

We must not be troubled by the fact that we see bad people enjoying great riches, while God's servants are reduced to the bare necessities. Brothers and sisters, we must have faith. We are competing in the contest of the living God, and we are in training in this present life so that we shall win our crown in the next.

(19, 20)

The Letters of Ignatius

To the Magnesians:
The Basic Choice in Life

All we do has an end, and we are faced with a choice between two things: death and life. We all shall go to our own proper place. And just as there are only two kinds of coinage, that of God and that of the world, each with its own character stamped upon it, so there are those without faith, who bear the imprint of this world, and there are those with faith, who bear in love the stamp of the Father through Jesus Christ.

If we do not choose to die through Christ in his passion, then his life will not be in us.

(5)

II
Living in Harmony with God

I urge you to try to do all things in harmony with God, under the presidency of the bishop, who holds the place of God, and of the presbyters, who hold the place of the college of apostles and of the deacons, who are so dear to me and who have been entrusted with the service of Jesus Christ, who was from eternity with the Father and was made manifest at the end of time.

Conform yourselves to God and have a deep respect for one another. Let no one look at another person according to the flesh, but in everything love one another in Jesus Christ.

Let there be nothing that might divide you, but be united with your bishop and with those who are set over you as an example and a lesson in things immortal.

(6)

III
Unity of the Body

Strive to be strong and firm in the things that the Lord and his apostles ordained for us. Then you will prosper in all you do, in mind and body, because you will be working from beginning to end in faith and love, in the Son and the Father and the Spirit, together with your revered bishop, the worthy crown of presbyters and the Godly deacons.

Submit yourselves to the bishop and to one another, as Jesus was subject to the Father and the apostles were subject to Christ and to the Father. In this way, it will be possible to have unity of spirit and of body.

(13)

To the Romans:
Dying to the World

I do not want you to please people but to please God, just as you please him now.

Never again shall I have such an opportunity of attaining God, nor shall you, if you keep silent, have a worthier deed attributed to you. For if you remain silent concerning me, then I am a word of God, but if you love my flesh, then once again I shall be only a meaningless cry.

Grant me nothing more than that I be poured out for God, while an altar is still ready. Thus, forming a chorus of love, you may sing to the Father in Christ Jesus that God by his favor has allowed the bishop of Syria to be found where the sun sets, having brought him there from where it rises.

It is good to die to the world, like the setting sun, so that I may rise again to him.

(2)

II
Christian Strength

You have never envied anyone, rather you have taught others. But I desire that those things you stress in your instructions should remain firm. Only pray for me for strength, both inward and outward, that I may not only speak with my tongue but also desire with my heart, that I may not only be called a Christian but also be found to be one.

For if I am found to be one, then I can also be called one and be faithful when I am no longer to be seen in the world.

(3)

III
God's Wheat

I am writing to all the Churches and issuing instructions to all that I am dying willingly for God and that you are not to hinder this. I beg you not to help me with untimely kindness. Let me be food for the wild beasts through whom I can come to God. I am God's wheat, and I am ground down by the teeth of wild animals, so that I may be made into the pure bread of Christ.

I would prefer you to entice the wild animals to become my tomb, leaving nothing of my bodily remains behind, so that I shall not be a burden to anyone after I am gone. Then I shall truly be a disciple of Jesus Christ, when the world can no longer even see my body.

Pray to Christ for me that I may be a worthy sacrifice through these instruments. I am not ordering you as did Peter and Paul, for they were apostles while I am a convict; they were free while I am still a slave. But if I suffer, I shall be Jesus Christ's own freedman, and in him I shall rise again in freedom.

What I am learning from my chains at present is not to desire anything.

(4)

IV
Dying and Living in Christ

The limits of the earth and the kingdoms of this world are worth nothing to me. It is better for me to die in Christ than to rule over the ends of the earth. My quest is for him who died for our sake; my desire is for him who rose again for us.

The pains of birth are upon me. Be indulgent toward me, friends. Do not prevent me from living, nor desire that I should die. Do not give to the world one who desires to belong to God, nor deceive him with material things. Allow me to receive the pure light; for when I have come to that light, my life as a man will have begun. Allow me to follow the example of the suffering of my God.

Anyone who has this God within them will understand my desire, and let them sympathize with me, knowing what it is that drives me on.

(6)

To the Philadelphians:
Unity Protection from Evil

So, as children of the light of truth, keep clear of division and wrong doctrine. You should run as sheep to where your shepherd is. For there is no lack of specious wolves who ensnare with corrupt pleasures those who run in God's race. But if you are united they will find no place among you.

(2)

II
Becoming Perfect for God

My brothers and sisters, my love for you is overflowing, and my joy is very great indeed as I watch over your safety. Though it is not I who do so, but Jesus Christ, whose bonds I bear, and I am all the more afraid in that I am not yet made perfect. But your prayer will make me perfect for God, so that I may attain the destiny that divine mercy has allotted me.

I shall take refuge in the gospel as in the flesh of Christ, in the apostles as in the Church's assembly of elders. And the prophets too we hold in affection, seeing that they also pointed clearly to the gospel, hoping and waiting in faith for the one who grants them salvation. Being in union with Jesus Christ, they are saints, deserving of our love and admiration and, approved by Jesus Christ, they are numbered with us in the gospel which is our common hope.

(5)

III
The Discernment of the Spirit

Even if some people wanted to deceive me in the flesh, the Spirit is not deceived, for it comes from God. It knows where it comes from and where it is going, and knows too how to test things that are hidden.

When I was with you, I cried out, I said with a very loud voice, with God's own voice: "Listen to the bishop, the presbyters and deacons." Some people suspected that I said these words with foreknowledge of the division that certain persons were going to cause. But the one I serve in chains is my witness that I had no knowledge of this from any human being.

It was the Spirit that was preaching, telling you this: "Do nothing without your bishop. Keep your flesh as the temple of God. Love unity. Avoid divisions. Be imitators of Jesus Christ, as he was of his Father."

(7)

IV
Christ, Basis of Faith

Therefore I did what I could as a man set on unity. God does not dwell where there is division and anger. The Lord forgives all who repent if they turn back to the unity of God and the advice of the bishop. I have faith in Jesus Christ, who will free you from all your chains.

But I urge you not to do anything in a spirit of divisiveness, but only according to the teaching of Christ. For I heard certain persons saying: "If I do not find it in the original documents of the Old Testament, then I do not believe it." And when I told them that it is indeed in scripture, they answered: "That is what we dispute."

For me, however, the original documents are Jesus Christ, the sacred original documents are his cross, his death, his resurrection and the faith we have through him, and it is in these that I desire to be justified by your prayers.

(8)

To the Smyrnaeans:
The Mind of God

Make no mistake, even the things in heaven and the glory of the angels, all rulers visible and invisible, face judgement if they do not believe in the blood of Christ. "He who is able to receive this, let him receive it." Let no one become puffed up because of the office they hold.

Faith and love are everything, to which nothing has been preferred. But note carefully those who hold unorthodox views concerning the grace of Jesus Christ which has come to us, how different they are from the mind of God. They are not concerned with love, with widows, orphans, the afflicted, those who have been imprisoned or released from prison, those who hunger or thirst.

(6)

To Polycarp:
Cherish Unity

Welcoming your mind which seems to be fixed in God as if on an immovable rock, I exult that I was found worthy to look upon your blameless face in which I hope to delight through God. I call upon you in the grace that you have received to pursue your present course and to urge all people to be saved. Justify your office by your efforts both physical and spiritual. Cherish unity, for there is nothing better. Help everyone, as the Lord helps you. Put up with everyone in love, as indeed you do. Devote yourself to prayers without end. Seek an increase in the wisdom you already have. Speak to each individual according to our common beliefs which come from God. Be alert and keep your spirit from falling asleep. Bear the sicknesses of all as a perfect athlete. Where the work is greatest, there is much to be won.

(1)

Words to Polycarp's Community

Listen well to your bishop and God will listen to you. I am devoted to those who are subject to the bishop, presbyters and deacons, and I pray that I may have my portion and part with them in God.

Work together, side by side, struggle together, run together, suffer together, rest together, rise up together as God's stewards, administrators and servants. Strive to please him in whose ranks you serve. It is from him that you will receive your pay.

Not one of you must be caught deserting. Let your baptism always be your weaponry, faith the helmet about your head, love your spear and endurance your armor. Lay up good deeds as a soldier deposits his savings, so that you can eventually receive the credit that is due to you.

Be patient with one another in gentleness therefore, as God is with you. May I have joy in you always.

(6)

The Letter of Polycarp
to the Philippians

Suffering for Christ

So let us persevere unceasingly in this hope that we have, and in the pledge of righteousness that is ours, Jesus Christ, "who bore our sins in his body on the tree, who committed no sin and in whose mouth there was no guile," but who endured all things for our sakes, so that we might have life in him.

Let us be imitators of his endurance then and, if we suffer for the sake of his name, let us glorify him. For this is the example that he set us in his own person, and in this we have believed.

(8)

A Prayer

I am quite sure that you are thoroughly versed in the scriptures and nothing is hidden from you. Unfortunately, I cannot say the same for myself. Only, as scripture has it: "Be angry but do not sin" and "Do not let the sun set while you are still angry."

Happy the person who keeps this message in mind, which I believe to be true in your case. May God, the Father of our Lord Jesus Christ, and the great eternal high priest himself, Jesus Christ the Son of God, make you strong in faith and truth and in all gentleness, without wrath, in patience and long-suffering, tolerance and chastity. May he give to you a part and a share in the lot of the saints and to us with you and to all under heaven who shall believe in our Lord and God, Jesus Christ, and in his Father who raised him from the dead.

Pray for all God's people. Pray also for emperors, princes and others in authority, for those who persecute you and hold you in contempt, and for those who are the enemies of the cross, so that your fruit may be seen by everyone and that you may be perfected in him.

(12)

The Letter to Diognetus

The Christian Life

It is not a particular kind of land or a particular kind of language or even a particular way of life that marks Christians out from their fellow human beings.

They neither have cities of their own nor speak a peculiar kind of dialect, nor do they have a way of life that is noticeably different from the norm. This doctrine of theirs is not one that has been invented by sharp and inquisitive minds, nor are they advocates of man-made dogma, as some people are.

Again, while they dwell in their several city-states up and down the Empire, whether Greek or not, each according to his or her appointed lot and following the local way of life in the matter of food and clothing and whatever else, they reveal the wonderful and undeniably strange character of their citizenship.

At home in their homelands, they are far from home. They share in all things as citizens, and suffer all things as total strangers. They get married as others do, and have children, but they do not expose their offspring. They will share their table with you, but not their marriage bed. They share the lot of all flesh, but not its fleshliness. On earth they walk; in heaven they live. They obey the appointed laws and surpass them in their own lives.

They love all people and are hunted down by all. They are unknown, yet publicly condemned. They are put to death, and yet gain life. Though poor, they make others rich. Lacking everything, they have an abundance of everything. They are dishonored, to their greater honor, and slandered to their credit.

When abused, they give blessing. When they do good, they are punished as if they did wrong, and being punished, they rejoice as people given new life. They are fought by the Jews as foreigners, and are persecuted by the Greeks—though those who hate them cannot say why.

(5)

Christians are the Soul of the World

In a word, what the soul is to the body is what Christians are to the world.

The soul is spread throughout all the members of the body, and so are Christians throughout the towns and cities of the world. The soul lives in the body, and yet it is not really part of the body. In the same way, Christians have their home in the world, and yet are not really of the world. The soul is an invisible thing, one that is confined within a visible body. So too are Christians seen to be in the world, yet their religion, their piety, remains invisible.

The flesh feels abhorrence for the soul and declares war upon it, even though it has not been harmed by it in any way, but simply because it is not given permission to wallow in its pleasures. In the same way, the world loathes Christians even though it has suffered no wrong from them, because they are opposed to its pleasures. The soul loves the flesh, which hates it, as Christians love those who hate them.

The soul is imprisoned in the body even though it sustains it, and Christians are contained in the world as in a prison, and yet they are the ones who sustain it. The undying soul makes its home in a body of death, and Christians sojourn in the midst of corruptible things in expectation of the incorruptibility which is in heaven.

The soul, if neglected in matters of food and drink, begins to make progress. And Christians too, when subjected to daily assaults, grow in numbers. It is to such a rank as this that God has assigned them, and they cannot properly decline it.

(6)

The Coming of Christ

As I said before, it is not some earthly discovery that has been handed down to Christians, nor is it some passing fancy or invention that they take such pains to preserve intact. Nor have they been entrusted with the guardianship of merely human mysteries. No, it was the almighty and unseen God of creation himself who placed the truth that comes from heaven in human hearts, and established there that sacred Word which no one can comprehend.

And this he did, not as you would expect through some servant or angel or ruler or someone appointed to the management of things on earth or in heaven, but through the very Architect and Creator of the universe. Through him it was that he made the heavens and enclosed the sea within its bounds, of whose mysteries all the elements of creation are the faithful guardians. From him it was that the sun received the measures of its appointed course, and it is at his command that the moon comes out at night. The stars too obey him as they follow in the moon's tracks, and it is by him that all things were set in order and put in their proper place—I mean the heavens and the sea, too, with all that it holds; fire, air, the great abyss; things in the heights, things in the depths, together with everything between them: he it was whom he sent to them.

But did he send him as we might suppose, with sovereign might and terror? Quite the contrary, it was in great gentleness, as a king sending his son, that he sent him as king, sent him as God, sent him as man to the human race—and all this to save and to persuade, without compulsion of any kind, because force and compulsion do not belong to God.

His sending was a call, not a pursuit. His sending was wholly love, not judgement.

Nevertheless, there will be a time when he will send him as judge too. And when that time comes, who is it that will endure his coming? Do you not see that they are thrown to wild beasts in order that they should deny the Lord, but are not conquered? Do you not see that the more of them that are punished, the more others join them? These things do not seem to be human works. These things are the wonders of God. These things are the proofs of his coming.

(7)

The Mercy of God

Although he had planned all things by himself to-gether with his Son, he allowed us up to the times that have preceded our own to be borne along by our rebellious drives just as we liked, carried away by our pleasures and appetites. It was not, of course, that he took delight in our sins, rather it was a question of forbearance. Nor was it that he condoned that period's evil, but rather he was preparing for this present period of good, so that we, who at that time had proved our-selves to be unworthy of life because of our own deeds, might now find the worthiness that comes from God, and we, who had so clearly shown ourselves incapable of entering God's kingdom by ourselves, might be given that possibility through that very power which is his own.

Now when our iniquity had had its fill and quite clearly the reward of punishment and death was awaiting it, there also came the time that God had awaited in order to display henceforth his goodness and his power (God is pure goodness, pure love!). In fact, he did not hate us, reject us or hold our sins against us. On the contrary, his patience was infinite, he tolerated us, and what is more, in his mercy he took our very sins upon himself, giving his own Son as a ransom for us. The Holy One he gave for the lawless, the Innocent for the guilty, the Just for the unjust, the Incorruptible for the corruptible, the Immortal for mortal creatures.

And what else was there that was capable of covering up our sins except his goodness? How could we ever have been considered just again, wicked and impious as we are, unless it was in God's only son, and in him alone? What a delightful exchange this is! What an unfathomable plan! What an unexpected kindness—that the wickedness of so many should be concealed in the goodness of one man, and that one man's justice should make many sinners just! Having convinced us therefore of the inability of our nature to attain life in the past, and having shown us the Savior who is capable of saving even where it is impossible, he wished on both accounts that we should believe in his goodness, regarding him as our nurse, father, teacher, advisor, healer, intelligence, light, honor, glory, strength, life, and that we should not worry about our food and clothing.

(9)

God's Imitators

God loved the human race and for our sake created the world, making all things on earth subject to us, giving us mind and the power to reason. It was on us alone that he placed the obligation of lifting our eyes up to him, whom he fashioned in his own image, to whom he sent his only-begotten Son, and to whom he promised the kingdom of heaven—and this he will give to those who have loved him.

And once you have this knowledge, do you know with what joy you shall be filled, or what love you will have for him who first loved you? By this love you will imitate his goodness. And do not be surprised that a human being can be the imitator of divinity; we can if God wants us to. For happiness does not lie in domination over our neighbors or in the desire to have more than the weak. Nor does it consist in having great riches and holding powers of coercion over poorer people. Nor is it in such ways that we can imitate God. On the contrary, such things are beyond the borders of his majesty.

But whoever lifts a neighbor's burden and carries it for them, whoever sees that they are better off in some respect than another less fortunate person and wants to help them, whoever gives those things they have received from God to the needy, such a person becomes a god to those who receive from them. And this person imitates God.

Then you will see, even while your lot has placed you on earth, that God has his dwelling-place in heaven; then you will begin to speak of God's mysteries; then you will love and admire those who suffer punishment for not wanting to deny God. Then, too, you will condemn the world's deceit and error, once you have learned of the true life in heaven, and have disregarded the seeming death of this world, fearing the death which is real and is reserved for those who are condemned to the eternal fire—the fire that will punish to the uttermost all those who were ever consigned to it. Then you will admire those who suffer the momentary fire for righteousness' sake, and once you have learned of that other conflagration, you will call them the most blessed of people.

(10)

Love and Knowledge

If you look carefully into these truths and listen attentively to them, you will know the kind of things that God bestows on those who love him in the right way. These are the people who have become a paradise of delight, raising up a flourishing and fertile tree within themselves, and they are thus adorned with all kinds of fruit.

Indeed, in this garden is planted the tree of knowledge and the tree of life. It is not, however, the tree of knowledge that kills, but rather, disobedience. The meaning of the written text is quite plain, namely, that God planted a tree of knowledge and a tree of life in the middle of paradise from the beginning, and showed that life comes through knowledge. But those who did not make a pure use of this life were in the very start stripped and deprived of it by the serpent's deceit. There is neither life without knowledge nor sound knowledge without true life. That is why we see them both planted together.

The apostle glimpsed the force of this and had strong words to say about the knowledge exercised separately and independently of the command that leads to life: "Knowledge puffs up, whereas love builds up." Anyone who thinks that they know a thing or two when they have nothing of that true knowledge which is borne out by a whole life's witness, in fact knows nothing at all. They are, on the contrary, under the serpent's spell, and do not love real life. But whoever has clear knowledge, tempered with fear, and is in search of life, plants in hope and believes that the fruit will come.

Let your heart be clear knowledge and your life the word of truth, fully absorbed. If you bear the tree associated with this and pluck its fruit, you will always be gathering in those very things that God himself longs to see—those things that are untouched by the serpent and untainted by deceit. In this case, Eve is not corrupted, but a virgin is trusted. Salvation is set forth, apostles are given understanding, the Lord's passover is brought nearer and the seasons are drawn together and harmonized with the world. The Word teaches his holy ones with great joy.

Through him the Father is glorified, to whom be glory for ever.

Amen.

(12)

Short Bibliography

Texts and Translations:

Lake, K. *Apostolic Fathers*. 2 vols. London, 1925.
Staniforth, M. (with additions by Andrew Louth). *Early Christian Writings*. Harmondsworth, 1987.

Studies:

Tugwell, S. *The Apostolic Fathers*. London, 1989.

Available in the same series:

GATEWAY TO PARADISE—BASIL THE GREAT

Edited by Oliver Davies
Introduction by A. M. Allchin
Translation by Tim Witherow

Basil the Great is one of the outstanding figures of the Eastern Church, an expert on spirituality. His writings have a universal appeal. They speak to people of all conditions and all times; perhaps, because they are filled with a deep and balanced faith, one which is aware of the majesty of God and of the beauty of the world.

It is characteristic of him that he is nearly always thought of in company, either as a member of his remarkable family which included his sister St. Macrina and his brother St. Gregory of Nyssa, or as one of a small group of thinkers, the Cappadocian Fathers, which included his friend St. Gregory Nazianzen.

He is very conscious of the need for solitude and silence, but also that the spiritual life can never be separated from inter-personal relationships. This is reflected in his fatherly concern to strengthen the community life of the newly-formed monastic groups of his time. Indeed, in relation to these his position in the East is very similar to that of St. Benedict in the West.

ISBN 1-56548-002-3, paper, 5 1/8 x 8, 128 pp.

Available in the same series:

BORN TO NEW LIFE—CYPRIAN OF CARTHAGE

Edited by Oliver Davies
Introduction by Cyprian Smith, O.S.B.
Translation by Tim Witherow

Cyprian of Carthage lived in troubled times. His freshness and topicality are in part due to this, because his world, as ours, was characterized by restlessness, insecurity and injustice. At the same time, his response to the world he lived in has a very modern tone because of his intense concern for the mystical life and for social justice.

But in one way he differs sharply from the outlook of today's world: in his other-worldliness. He is very much aware that everything will pass away, and that the present life has value only in a larger perspective.

Possibly here, as much as where he shares contemporary attitudes, he has a great deal to pass on to us, and we can learn to live the new life he experienced if we listen attentively to him telling of his discoveries.

ISBN 1-56548-006-6, paper, 5 1/8 x 8, 128 pp.